THE
SHIFTING
WEB

ALSO BY LEWIS TURCO

THE SHIFTING WEB

NEW AND SELECTED POEMS

Lewis Turco

The University of Arkansas Press
Fayetteville   London   1989

Designer: Chiquita Babb
Typeface: Linotron 202 Janson
Typesetter: G & S Typesetters, Inc.
Printer: Braun-Brumfield, Inc.
Binder: Braun-Brumfield, Inc.

The paper used in this publication meets the minimum re-
quirements of the American National Standard for Perma-
nence of Paper for Printed Library Materials Z39.48-1984. ∞

Library of Congress Cataloging-in-Publication Data

Turco, Lewis.
    The shifting web : new and selected poems, 1957–1989 /
Lewis Turco.
        p.   cm.
    ISBN 1-55728-090-8 (alk. paper). — ISBN 1-55728-091-6
(pbk. : alk. paper)
    I. Title.
    PS3570.U626.S48   1989
    811'.54–dc19   89-4675
                                                           CIP

To the memory of
John Ciardi
poet, mentor, friend

Acknowledgments

The author owes thanks to the publishers of the following volumes from which these poems have been selected:

First Poems, Golden Quill Press (1960); *The Sketches of Lewis Turco and Livevil: A Mask*, American Weave Press (1962); *Awaken, Bells Falling: Poems 1959– 1967*, University of Missouri Press (1968); *The Inhabitant*, Despa Press (1970); *Pocoangelini: A Fantography and Other Poems*, Despa Press (1971); *The Weed Garden*, Peaceweed Press (1973); *A Cage of Creatures*, Banjo Press (1978); *Seasons of the Blood*, Mammoth Press (1980); *American Still Lifes*, Mathom Publishing Company (1981); *The Compleat Melancholick*, The Bieler Press (1985); and *A Maze of Monsters*, Livingston University Press (1986).

Of the pieces in the section of new poems, "The Habitation" was published as a broadside by the Bellevue Press (1978); "The Recurring Dream" appeared in *The Hudson Review;* "The Girl You Thought You Loved" in *Modern Poetry Studies;* "Vigilance" in *Ploughshares;* "Attic Poem" and "Cancer" in *The Sewanee Review;* "A Daughter Moves Out" in *The University of Windsor Review;* "Reflections at Forty-Nine" and "Conceit" in *Voices in Italian Americana;* and "Poem" in *Poetry Northwest.*

"An Ordinary Evening in Cleveland," "The Schooner," and "The Trestle" appeared originally in *The New Yorker.*

"Awaken, Bells Falling," "Death," "Home Thoughts," "The Kitchen," "The Mill" (under the title "The Villagers"), "Pocoangelini 5," "Pocoangelini 7," and "The Scythe" appeared originally in *Poetry.*

Contents

from *First Poems,*
Awaken, Bells Falling: Poems 1959–1967,
& *The Weed Garden*

from *The Sketches,*
Pocoangelini: A Fantography and Other Poems,
The Inhabitant,
& Seasons of the Blood

from *American Still Lifes*

from *A Cage of Creatures* & *A Maze of Monsters*

from *The Compleat Melancholick*

New Poems

FROM

First Poems,

Awaken, Bells Falling:
Poems 1959–1967,

& The Weed Garden

A Dedication

for John Brinnin and Don Justice,
on a line by Joel Sloman

          If it is true that
"the sea worm is a decorated flute
          that pipes in the most ancient mode"—
          and if it is true, too, that
the salt content of mammalian blood
          is exactly equivalent
to the salinity of the oceans
at the time life emerged onto the land;

          and if it is true
that man is the only mammal with a
          capacity for song, well, then,
          that explains why the baroque
worm swims in our veins, piping, and why
          we dance to his measure inch by
equivocal inch. And it explains why
this song, even as it explains nothing.

Street Meeting

I saw him on the street.
His flesh was heavy.
For years we had not met:
Time takes its levy,
Returning ounce for hour.
But the eyes I'd known
Had stayed the same though flesh constricted bone.

His eyes owned all the past—
I saw it staring,
Bewildered, not at rest,
Still full of daring,
But fettered now by the hoar
of revolving clocks:
A hurt, unlikely witch within its stocks.

I watched the troubled look
His face reflected
And knew he'd pick my lock
Had time defected.
But each of us could hear
Wary sentries call
And answer in the long, resounding hall.

We spoke in platitudes,
      Each of us helpless,
The victims of our moods
      And of our losses:
The present was the heir
                  Of our common past.
The future would inherit all at last.

We parted. Each of us
      Had fanned an ember.
We'd shared another loss
      And would remember.
But time was still for hire:
                  He walked off alone.
When next we meet our prisons will have grown.

Visitor

Visitor, you've come and you've gone while I was
gone, while winds were moving through open windows,
billowing the drapes in my vacant chambers,
        sounding the silence;

come and gone, whoever you were, and left no
note but quiet sliding among the shadows.
Here before my house, by the stolid doorway,
        I remain watching,

listening where you must have lingered, waiting.
I stand listening for the bell's thin echo,
knowing for a certainty you were here and
        left without echo.

All will turn out differently now. Behind this
door there stands an alien future. Words that
needed speaking have not been spoken, and the
        time that has not been

spent correctly now must be handled strangely,
sold less truly, used in another manner.
Sounds have not been breasted. The stillness thickens
        over your footfalls.

Visitor, between us are tunnels sealed and
hollow; there are depths where once there were crossings.
There are windows, too, gone opaque with wonder,
        darkling with questions.

My Country Wife

My country wife bends to rinse. Her skirt is
    unwrinkled. Its print of flowers rounds
out her womb like the rug of violets
        that mounds or dimples the chapel
burying ground. She would be grotesque where
        hydrants irrigate gutters.

Here, she is a sleight of the moon; the sound
        a mole makes. She bends and carries. She
cooks and smiles her meals down my throat. I need
        no teeth. She has done what the bee
does to clover. The sun moves around. She
        stays and stays. She sweeps and cooks.

The Townsfolk

There is, first, the road,
which goes nowhere out of
nowhere endlessly. And beside
it, beside the road, grass
and flowers growing, some trees,

leaves covered with dust.
A barn stands caught in a
twist of the road, paint peeling in
the insensible sun.
Somewhere a dove mourns under

eaves. A phoebe calls
out the season crisply,
and the townsfolk move out of no-
where, walking, going no-
where with birdcalls and flowers.

An Old Acquaintance

As we stand talking, his eye
    drops out. I am amazed.
    His socket looks funny.
    It's a nice day, I say.
His scalp is scattered on the

carpet. What's the matter with
    your nose, I ask—but it
    is too late. He laughs. His
    teeth hit something on their
way down. I must be getting

on, I suggest. But I am
    too slow to catch his ear.
    Can't you say something? I
    inquire: he opens his
mouth to show me. That's too bad,

I say, but he shakes his head
    too hard. I try looking
    into his mind, but he
    is thinking of nothing.
A spider is spinning her

web in a white cave. It is
    awkward. Well, it's getting
    late, I say. The spider
    has caught something. I smile
at him; he stands there grinning.

Millpond

Yaddo, Saratoga Springs, New York

This is the place where peace grows
like a green frond set among waters aerial
      with dragonflies. Where, at noon,
the trees section the broad falling
leaf of light, and space color upon the millpond,
      yet do not move because motion
         might be lost upon silence.

This is the place where a stone,
given its occasional career, could disturb
      little with an arc and fall,
for the pond would swallow all voice
and shrug circling ripples into its banks until
      moss had absorbed this small wet gift,
         showing a fancy darker.

This is the place where one may
abet his heart's romance, deceiving his eyes by
      unconsciously confusing
slow change with no change. But even
here, dream makes way for declensions of wind and sun.
      The alders will grow, moss will dry.
         Wings will pulsate, then plummet.

This is the place where peace rests
like ferns beyond lilies. The trick is to wear it
as a mantle, but to know
cloaks for cloaks, shelters for shelters.
Beneath this reverie of surfaces, fish wait
for the dragonfly's mistake. The
trick is to lose, but to own.

School Drawing

There is a road: no
one is walking there. Brown
paper, black paper triangles
wrangle with the air
to make a windmill

striping a crayon
sun. A black arrow points
away from the blades that turn in
fire. It is burning,
and there is no wind.

An Ordinary Evening in Cleveland

I

Just so it goes: the day, the night—
what have you. There is no one on TV;
  shadows in the tube, in the street.
In the telephone there are echoes and mumblings,
  the buzz of hours falling thru wires.

And hollow socks stumbling across
the ceiling send plaster dust sifting down
  hourglass walls. Felix the cat has
been drawn on retinas with a pencil of light.
  I wait gray, small in my cranny,

for the cardboard tiger on the
kitchen table to snap me, shredded, from
  the bowl.

II

Over the trestle go
the steel beetles grappled tooth-and-tail—over and
  over and over there smokestacks

lung tall hawkers into the sky's
spittoon. The street has a black tongue: do you
  hear him, Mistress Alley, wooing
you with stones? There are phantoms in that roof's trousers;
  they kick the wind. The moon, on a

ladder, is directing traffic
now. You can hardly hear his whistle. The
oculist's jeep wears horn rim wind
shields; the motor wears wires on its overhead valves—
grow weary, weary, sad siren,

you old whore. It's time to retire.

III
The wail of the child in the next room quails
like a silverfish caught in a
thread. It is quiet now. The child's sigh rises to
flap with a cormorant's grace through

the limbo of one lamp and a
slide-viewer in your fingers: I cannot
get thin enough for light to shine
my color in your eyes; there is no frame but this for
the gathering of the clan. Words

will stale the air. Come, gather up
our voices in the silent butler and
pour them into the ashcan of
love. Look, my nostrils are dual flues; my ears are
the city dump; my eyes are the

very soul of trash; my bitter
tongue tastes like gasoline in a ragged
alley.

IV
The child cries again. Sounds
rise by the riverflats like smoke or mist in time's
bayou. We are sewn within seines

of our own being, thrown into
menaces floating in shadows, taken
without volition like silver
fish in an undertow down the river, down time
and smog of evenings.

V
The child cries.

VI
Do you hear the voice of wire?
Do you hear the child swallowed by carpets,
the alley eating the city,
rustling newsprint in the street begging moonlight with
a tin cup and a blindman's cane?

VII
The lamps are rheumy in these tar
avenues. Can you sense the droppings of
flesh falling between walls falling,
the burrowings of nerves in a cupboard of cans?
Can you hear the roar of the mouse?

VIII
There is nothing but the doorway
sighing; here there is nothing but the wind
swinging on its hinges, a fly
dusty with silence and the house on its back buzzing
with chimneys, walking on the sky

like a blind man eating fish in an empty room.

The Old Professor and the Sphinx

It is a dry word in a dry book
drying out my ear. I squat and swallow
my tongue here in this chair,
the desert of my desk, summer bare, spreading
like a brown horizon into regions grown arid
with erudition. A caravan of books treks

stolidly across my eyes while I,
the Sphinx, a phoenix nesting in my skull,
pry into inkwells and
gluepots seeking the universal solvent.
There is none. The pages as I turn them sound like sand
rattling in the sec temples of a beast gone to

earth with the sun. I lie caught in my
creaking dune, shifting with the wind of the
pharaohs, wondering if,
somewhere, I have not missed my valley. Upon
the walls of my office there are Oriental prints
hanging stiff as papyrus, whispering their brown

images into the silent air.
I know the poems on my shelves speak with
one another in an
ancient language I have somehow forgotten.
If there is rainfall, I recall, the desert blossoms—
but I have somewhere lost the natural prayer

and instinctual rites of the blood
which can conjure clouds in seasons of drought.
There is but ritual
remaining; no honey is in the lion's
hide; my temples have mumbled to ruin: they endure
disuse and despair. An archaeologist of

cabinets and drawers, I exhume
paperclip skeletons, the artifacts
of millennia: red.
ball-point pens with nothing in their veins, pencils
like broken lances, and notebook citadels empty
of citizens—the crusader has squandered his

talents on bawds, grown hoary in their
service. The town is sacked: the bawds are gone
to tame younger legions.
Look into my sarcophagus: the tapes are
sunken over my hollow sockets. Slowly the waste
swallows my oasis like a froth of spittle.

The Forest Beyond the Glass

Hundreds of yards of woodland
smashed and torn.
They had been a long while dying,
these great beasts;
one, of a broken neck—the lucky
one. Thirst took
the other: even on his side he'd dug
a dozen

holes, deep as his hooves could delve,
trying for
water. It had been one of those
tremendous
agonies. There lie the two moose still,
locked upon
love's combat, horns fused. All is as it was.
The bulls are

dead; so says the placard hung
upon the
glass; thus they were found, silent in
the forest.
The point and object of contention
had long since
vanished when men happened upon these hulks
steaming in

a spring thaw. But it was not
love that had
conquered; as usual, it was
time. Engrossed
with death's petrified grove and with the
heart's beasts calm
in the wildwood, we stand frozen by love's
passing glance
reflected in the forest beyond the glass.

Burning the News

The fire is eating
the paper. The child who drowned
is burned. Asia is in flames.
As he signs his great
bill, a minister of state chars

at the edges and curls
into smoke. The page rises,
glowing, over our neighbor's
roof. In the kitchens
clocks turn, pages turn like gray wings,

slowly, over armchairs.
Another child drowns, a bill
is signed, and the pen blackens.
The smoke of Asia
drifts among the neighbors like mist.

It is a good day for burning.
The fire is eating the news.

Awaken, Bells Falling

It is a dawn quick as swallows
        peeling to shear through peals belled
from the one town steeple. Autumn
falls from green heat like a chestnut felled
out of its prickly jacket. A single

jay walks in the pines. A cone of
        cold sweeps chill's needles soughing
through the day's screen doors. There can be
no cushioning today: to wake
shall be a sharp thing. The person on his

private ticking will be palsied
        from his sheets, his numeral
be rung, the coils of consciousness
spring him into good woolen light,
without armament, to meet himself in

mirrors and still halls. Meet himself—
        find his blood walking a thin
line, alarums unsleeping him.
Brazen as flame leaving ash for
the elm's sere leaf, autumn will have settled

into summer's pallet—patchwork
and quilting: that poor thread of
dreams curling at the doorsill. It
is done, the keen tone spoken, wrung
out of the bronze tongue of silence. Winter;

allcolor; whiteness. Who will braid
our years now into what skein
of circles? Bells fail in the streets;
the hall empties us into ice,
sheeted, sheer as mirrors, unreflecting.

Home Thoughts

Time buzzes in the ear. Somewhere
nearby, beyond my peripheral
vision, an insect throbs its heartsong
to the couch. A twilleter fuzzes
    against a burning lamp. Outdoors,

    a common goatsucker strings twelve
yellow streetlamps on its bill. Between
its hoarse shrieks, the town sky drops pieces
of clum among my snoring neighbors.
    If I close my eyes, a crack along

    the wall comes sliving my lids to
split the mind's dry sight. Look inward: a
plaster skull sifts dust down upon old
webs that hang, buzzing, as darkness moves
    ruthlessly to feast on something

small and hollow with blind, jeweled eyes.

Lovers

The bed frames them. Their eyes
tell little of the story. Some old passion
has been eroded. Rivulets of time have
    eaten their cheeks until their faces

    lie flat against linen
landscapes—or against each other in a dark
room, on a night empty even of owlcries.
    Their flesh is a sophistry of shadow:

    nothing is hidden. They
must therefore film their eyes in order not to
notice there is nothing there to see. They sang
    songs once, to each other, in moon light.

    Now, not even night hawks
call out to the lovers in their still stead. Not
even sleep lifts the veils from their sight, returns
    each other's image for an hour's dream.

        And if the world wheel, what then?
      The grim creature of the mind stunned
by the spaces of stars hung silently
    among the dumb regions where death dwells
in an old house, watching from twin windows,

snuttering among pebbles
    like a hag made of pimples and
sacks. She will stow her hours in odd chinks,
    fondle each old thing on her ticking
as night whines beneath the bed and her roof

        trembles with light. Then, at last,
    when least she needs his flesh—when least
they know each other in their age, the stars
    will smash their windows, their roof vanish,
and the world come burning while they make love.

The Weed Garden

I am the ghost of the weed garden.
    Stalk among stones—you will find me
remembering husks and pods, how crisp burdock
  couches in the moon for every passer.
    I am the dry seed of your mind.

    The hour will strike when you dream me, your
      hand at the sheet like five thin hooks.
I will wait for you in the old vines rattling on
  the wind, in the ground-pine. I will show you
    where rue has blossomed and eyebright,

    mother-thyme. You must name me Yarrow.
    Bitter vetch shall catch your step as
you follow, hearing the stars turning to crystal,
  sweet lovage turning sere, adder's tongue and
    Jew's-ear at their whisper. Nightshade

    will consume the beautiful lady.
    Dwarf elder, dodder-of-thyme, I
am the thing you fear in the simple of your blood:
  toothwort in the dust, feverfew, mouse-ear,
    sundew and cup-moss, tormentils.

Mary Moody Emerson, R.I.P.

for Hyatt H. Waggoner

        Ralph Waldo's Aunt Mary,
   moody as all getout, got herself
      rigged out in a shroud and rode
      through Concord on a donkey
"to get herself in the habit of the

        "tomb." Ralph Waldo, though she
  wore her cerements daily ever
      after, reckoned her beast of
      burden was more symbolic
than her garb. If he could transcend Calvin,

        concordantly, why not
  she? Ceremonies of Innocence
      and Hope lay everywhere be-
      fore her grave step, were she but
to look: "There grow the Leaves of Grass." *But what*

       makes them so green? "On the
  village square a concourse of elms praises
      the good Lord." *In their shadow*
      the moss grows. "All are Elect!"
Then why so few who can see? Ralph Waldo

        shrugged and put down to whim this
  relative moodiness. When they put
      her down at last in her life-
      long weeds, Ralph Waldo blessed her
blind eyes as, no doubt, Aunt Mary blessed his.

The Pilot

Calais, France, May 18, 1968 (AP)—Low tide
yesterday uncovered a plane, presumably of
World War II, with the remains of the pilot
still at the controls. Its origin could not be
determined immediately.

It has been
a long flight. Like flak,
the seagrass exploded
beneath me as I fell
out of light into
an older and a heavier air.

My planing
continued in the tide.
When the scavengers had
done with my flesh, I found
that still the stick would
answer, though more slowly than before.

So I flew,
and am flying still, back
to the beginning. In
my marrow direction
lay. Now the sea has
released me, and I have been constant.

But I was
wrong. You see me at death's
controls, in the primal
mud where our flight began,
but it has not been
a fleeing, as we have long supposed.

30

I see that
now, with these sockets where
fish have swum. You, rising
from the shore, have shown me
what the snail tried to
tell: the journey is the other way.

Turn me around. I am with you still.

Tick

I am a cat with a tick
buried in my head. If I could speak,
    I would tell you I can feel
the insect head nestling within my

    brain, not just against the white
bone. I can sense its mechanical
    currents buzzing in the blood,
showing the mandibles how to clench,

    the belly how to bloat, how
to make two lives one. It is not a
    matter of will for either:
It feels my claws sliding in their sheaths;

    I feel it growing stronger
on my substance.
                        My master?
As he looks at us, I see our two

    minds sink into his eyes. We three
meet at the center of his thoughts. My
    claws unsheath there. The insect
bloats in dark vessels. Here is where we

shall live together—a nest
of boxes, three separate designs,
three steps in Becoming, a
skull within a skull within a skull.

The Dream

This is the story of a dream:
the gas station in a poor location,
    shadowed, even in daylight. The cars
           on their great tires—the twenties
or early thirties. But not many

      on the road. Perhaps evening is
coming on, darkness moving in, an air
    of something waiting in the gas pumps,
          behind the cooler. It is
summer. I am in attendance. If

      the lights were on perhaps someone
might turn off the road, drive up the old tar,
    ride over the sparse grass in the cracks,
         stop there, outside the dusty
window where I stand watching. Then, with

      the thought, they are there—four of them
getting out of the square sedan. As they
    come filing toward the door, heads turned,
         looking at me through the hard
glass with their hard eyes, I know there is

      no way out. They'll find no money,
though—something in me grins at the thought, and

the thought worries it. They are staring
at me: the first is nearly
at the door. As our eyes lock I am

shocked by the pistol in his hand,
by the flame in the muzzle, the shattered
glass, by my blindness as the bullet
enters the brain where I know
I am lost and reeling, blood pouring

between my fingers, bathing my
eyes, and no sensation of pain, only—

a vague regret that I will
now accomplish no more; certainty

that this is death; amazement that
I can think with a shattered brain; knowledge
that if I wake again they will
have saved me; rejection of
the possibility. But beyond

these and above them: immense joy.
It is over. It is nothing—nothing
I could have imagined. Mere joy, great
relief, release, and silence.
And I awake, but cannot believe

in waking. It has not happened,
yet nothing more real has ever happened.
Stumbling out of my blood into this
walking dream, nothing is left
except these words, images of weed,

dust, flame in a dark cylinder, and joy.

FROM

The Sketches,

Pocoangelini:
A Fantography and Other Poems,

The Inhabitant,

& *Seasons of the Blood*

Louie the Barber

Up the block, all you kids,
    it's time for the shearing of hairs;
    it's the day the sun makes Saturday,
    church day tomorrow; it's the day
    baldy Lou, he of the lollipops,
    lowers the boom on your cowlicks and locks.
No pied piper, he: behind his chair
    he's gleeman, however, once you're inside
    with your nose a trunkful of pomade smells,
    Vitalis, Wild Root Cream Oil, Charlie.
Is it baseball you're missing?
Are the bats thwacking in the back lot
    while you bend your head and want to scratch,
    and the scissors snip and the mirror
    near the chair beckons you to move just once?
"Well, the Yanks won," says Louie, "yes, the Yanks
    won and the Sox lost and what grade you in
    now, sonny?
"Steady now, steady your head, one more swipe
    of the comb—wish
    I could comb *my* hair," says Louie,
    "See?"—
The bald head lowered to pat, the chuckle,
    "*Bene, bene*, go home now, you're done,
    next man, who's next?

"Who's next?" says Louie.

Lorrie

Lorrie looked good—man,
    she was a jazz band, straight
    as a clarinet, and the tunes she played
    with her hip action wowed my crowd.
Lorrie swung like a prime ensemble,
    smiled the cool blues as we sipped our
    brews in the racetrack dive while the
    bass thrummer, a basic type, swiped
    at the strings, making us think
    of beds and things.
There we were, dancing our eyes
    among the beers while Lorrie walked
    her pert way among us, mashers all,
    and we asked, "What's up tonight,
    Lorrie-love?"
"I've no time," she smiled, "no time—
    I'm a college girl, my major's law.
"By night I slide drinks down
    to your hands, and in the daylight
    I guard lives at Ryall's beach."
Then, when the jazz bunch quit and
    the horn stopped snorting
    and the drums bumped the last bum
    out the door, we went too, man,
    we went too.

Who wants to see Lorrie meet her beau?
    Who wants to see his old eyes, older
    than she'll ever be, and his dark hands
    grab her wrist hard as they leave to park
    in the raceway woods?

Bordello

Hank Fedder

Hank Fedder is my name. My wife is Maud
Fedder—she's a good woman, the neighbors
say. And she is, I guess. She's sure no bawd,
and that's God's truth. Goodness just about pours
out of her. Depends on what you call "good,"
of course. She's *good* in the house, out of doors,
at market, in her clubs—just anyplace.
Except in bed. There, she rubs my face

in the "dirt" she calls my "male mind." She makes
me sick of myself, of what I need to
do. She cuts my guts out, and then she takes
what's left of me, sets it in the window
like a dummy, calls it "Hubby," "Dad," bakes
cakes for it, and sends it off to work. Oh,
yes, she's good all right. She makes a fine spouse.
On her bridge night I come to this whorehouse

to salvage what's left of my need, of my
insides. It never works. I leave here done
to death with sickness, the sickness that I
have now, truly, just as she claims. She's won
her point. I'm not the man she married by
a long shot—no man at all. And my son,
our son . . . he knows it, hates the "hubby" of
that best of mothers he will always love.

42

Jasper Olson

I take my women any way they come—
I'm Jasper Olson, brother. Hard and fast
I play this game. Though some folks think I'm dumb,
I take my women any way they come,
and come they do. There's no time to be numb
in this life—grab it now and ram the past.
I take my women any way they come.
I'm Jasper Olson, brother, hard and fast.

Jonathan Hawkins

For as many nights as there are
days in the month, I come here to
sleep with a woman. The first star
sees me climb the hill, for my cue
is a point of light—oddly, you
may think. But the light floats upon
a vast shadow. My name is Jon
Hawkins . . . Jonathan, but none call
me that. I come here and knock on
this door that opens. And that's all,

or almost. It is not far
to climb the hill from the town. Few
people see me, not that I care
anyway. I'm past all that. Two
or three townsfolk might stick their blue
noses in the air still. I'm stone
to them. The old Hawkins mansion
was sold years back. Few would recall
my father, *or* my father's son.
This door that opens (and that's all)

43

opens for a wastrel. A jar
full of fireflies, an untrue
flame—that's this house to me: the instar
that never became a moth, who
was born but not transformed. I grew,
yes, but not enough. What makes one
man want to try to reach the sun;
another, want a candle? Tall
he was, my father. He would shun
this door that opens. And that's all

my story. Still . . . I am *not* done.
I come here to win what is won
easily, and I cannot fall
far. I touch, out of my dungeon,
this door that opens, and that's all.

Will Somers

The sun shone all day
like a bright cock preening
for its hen. Making hay
lay over the greening
grass. There is no meaning
hidden for you to trace
in these wishes leaning
like moonlight on my face,

for I live as I may—
I, Will Somers—gleaning
in all weathers. I say,
"lay over the greening
world well, the wind keening
or soughing." Woman's grace

is but a night's dreaming,
like moonlight on my face:

a thing met with on the way,
taken without scheming.
I never married. Clay
lay over the greening
sap of my youth. Steaming
nights I spent alone; lace
fancies all went streaming
like moonlight on my face,

like sweat. Sweat, careening,
lay over the greening
fields. Now, I know love's place,
like moonlight on my face.

Simon Judson

In this dark place I am still with God.
Here I read the pages of man's lust,
seek the revelation of the sod,
remind the flesh again, "Thou art dust."

I am not of this town. Reverend
Mister Simon Judson is my name,
and my parish is down at the end
of Route 40, miles away. I came
here first just about a year ago—
accidentally, of course. I must
be honest; I would not go a rod
for sensual satisfaction. No,
I come to this house because I must
seek the revelation of the sod,

not because my life is cold. I lend
my soul to my flock weekly. The same
is true *in re* my family. To mend
my spirit, I renew it in shame
at the fount of blood, as the saints do.
I drive long distances, for great blame
would attend me were I found out. Trust
and good faith are my stock in trade, so
I spare no pains to avoid a nod,
remind the flesh again, "Thou art dust,"

and keep peace. Even my closest friend
might not understand my pilgrim aim.
This sinful hovel is a Godsend,
truly. Here all the worst vices flame
out of the Pit for my study—glow
and glitter like Sodom. That I know
man's follies firsthand is fact—disgust
and degradation; the mire, the rust
of will—here I am armored and shod!
Here I read the pages of man's lust . . . .
In this dark place I am still with God.

Rick de Travaille

Having fallen down the manhole,
I discovered myself to be
in the wrong world. Having no soul
was a problem at first for me,

but I, Rick de Travaille, ignore
the problem now. I split this door
where the women are, and I find
in the flesh a little peace of mind.

Jason Potter

Suddenly, nothing was left of all those
years we'd spent together in the same house,
under that old mansard that bent and rose
above us, gracefully guarding. The spruce

in the dooryard spired out of the grass
like a steeple, pulling us taut as bows—
both generations. But age is a noose:
suddenly, nothing was left of all those

mornings and nights. I, Jason Potter, chose
to lay away my helpmeet and my spouse
in a lone bed. So ended my repose.
Years we'd spent together in the same house

became beads to tell, the string broken—loose
time come unstrung. Still, outside, the spruce grows,
and it is nature to try to mend loss.
Under that old mansard that bent and rose

over the life we'd built, my blood still flows
in fever now and then. I make my truce
with flesh through these paid women whom I use.
Above us, guarding and graceful, the spruce

used to seem a symbol of common use
and fulfillment of self and heart—those blues
tipping sheer limbs sharply; strong and close
and clean, the bole and needles of pure hues . . . .
Suddenly, nothing was left.

Lafe Grat

In this house I am not ugly—nowhere
else. Nor is there
a mirror in the room we use, my bought
bride and I. What
images are reflected in her eyes
I recognize
as in a dream only, my face redrawn
by night. Reborn
each evening of this woman, spared my name,
the cruel fame
of the publicly disfigured, I roar
with my old whore
like a whole man, transfigured for a time.
Sordid? I am
Lafe Grat. I work hard to make a living.
There's no giving
to a man who makes you think of darkness,
for my likeness
is found buried in everyone, hidden
till, unbidden,
it rises to gorge the beast in the blood.
So, out of mud
I am formed and rise each morning to stalk
where others walk
in a world of surfaces—till night when,
like other men,
I may purchase with coin my manhood, life—
a moment's wife.

Envoi: The Wind Carol

The townspeople peer out of their windows—
the black snow falls, and the wind blows.

From each imprisoning flake that falls
an image looks out at the walls
of faces, and a thin voice calls
to the townspeople peering out of their windows.

Melisande comes drifting down
out of the air above the town,
recalling the lace of her wedding gown,
the years like snow in the wind that blows.

The Captain falls, epaulettes gleaming,
through a pine where the wind's streaming
rustles, then rises like missiles screaming
toward the enemy's thin windows.

These are cold voices that comprise
this dark wind touching a storm of eyes—

Mary, trapped in her bit of hoar,
gazes out of her dim mirror
thinking of lovers outside her door
lashing, like limbs, in the wind that blows.

Old Tom remembers some fleeting kiss
which he'd thought lost, but was caught like this
within his mind's paralysis
of moments frozen behind windows.

And as it falls or drifts, each face,
stunned in an attitude of grace
or of despair, looks for its place
among its kind in the wind that blows.

These are cold voices that comprise
this dark wind touching a storm of eyes.
The townspeople peer out of their windows;
the black snow falls, and the wind blows.

Pocoangelini 1

Pocoangelini sat
astride a seahorse singing.
The moon rode a wave beside him.
"Moon" he sang "O moon O moon O,
I am Pocoangelini."

Upon a wave beside him
rode the moon. Tangled in weed
it sang, "Pocoangelini,
Poco Poco Angelini
I am a white dove of the night."

Pocoangelini sang
and the moon sang. The seahorse
bridled each wave, and the sea shied.
"O Moon O Poco Moon" they sang,
"Angelini, dove of the night."

Pocoangelini 5

Pocoangelini said,
"Lady, the bell is on my cap,
the cap is upon this head.
Womanhood wound in roses and ivy
shall never understand me."

To him she did reply,
"I have heard the bell upon your cap,
and, with my own eye,
sir, have I perceived its bobble.
It is a pretty bauble."

Then did Angelini shake
his sceptre into the blowing moon
there, where the trees make
spires of shadow into the night.
But his eyes were bright.

Sweet, the lady's laughter
rang to the bell's jangle. A bird,
caught in a limb, softer
echoed her joy out of the wood—
then he understood.

"Lady," did Poco cry,
"you misperceive my good intent
and the brightness of my eye.
My dance is light, the moon is pure,
this bell is *not* a lure!"

"Sir," then said the lady,
"though I may not *apprehend* you,
these are shadows, never ivy.
Let the bell sing, for the moon shows
that your sceptre is the rose."

Pocoangelini 7

Pocoangelini: Sir. Your head. It is stuck into the sand.
Mr. Earth:

Pocoangelini: I'm not sure I understand. You hear me,
don't you, even with both your earholes squat
up against those furrows? I say, YOUR HEAD
IS STUCK IN A BRAIN'S HARROWING. There's dirt
up your nose and ants are crawling about
your neck. YOUR HEAD'S STUCK IN THE FILTHY SAND!
Mr. Earth:

Pocoangelini: The moon is out. It's playing with your spine.
The shafts of starfire are sticking in your
shoulderblades, making you appear to be
a sort-of celestial porcupine. What
are you looking for? What color is the
inside? Have you found whether stones push each
other when they are together alone?
Mr. Earth:

Pocoangelini: Look, I'll scoop you out so we can talk like
human beings. It's a cold night. Your thoughts
must be chilly. This is no hour for such
silver. I'll dig. Now pull, and tell me . . . .

Mr. Earth:

Pocoangelini: Oh!

Pocoangelini 8

The first thing in the morning
Pocoangelini took
the babe a candle. "Here is
a candle," he said, "for your stable."

But the mother said, "No, no.
Here there is too much straw." So
Pocoangelini took it back,
brought in its stead some honey dew. "Oh,"

said the mother, "no. My milk
is better for the baby's
eating. Take away your dew."
So Pocoangelini bargained

in the marketplace. He gave
the child a singing, jeweled
bird. "Ah," the mother said, "that
shall do well enough. Its song will lull

my babe to sleep, my child to
sleep. Emerald eyes shall keep
green watch above his slumber."
"And there shall fall from its beak,"

said Pocoangelini,
"a comforter of shadow—
black bunting for your baby.
For David's star on a golden cross

"candle light and honey dew,
black bunting for your baby."

Pocoangelini 12

She is caught in her frail house
as Poco is caught in his. The rib she stole
is the furniture of his breast. Poco puts
his ear to listen to the nameless Word
her lung suspires into blood, and the word
redounds, echoes out of the breath
of his own mouth.

                    Listen. She would have
seed of Pocoangelini. She would bring
more bone forth to walk among the walkers,
to chisel rimes upon monuments
in the fields among groves and grass—
the boudoir where lovers lie at last.

Pocoangelini 26

In the empty stadium he stood
   in the batter's box
swinging at balls that weren't there.
Whiff! "Strike twelve," said Pocoangelini.
   The empty bleachers roared.

No one on the mound wound up and pushed
   a fast one past him.
Pocoangelini furrowed
the air, the bat whistling in the dust, sun
   scorching his cap's visor.

"Strike twenty, twenty-one," Poco said
   and stopped to rest. Then,
again, he swung and swung and swung
at nothing. "Fifty, fifty-one," he said.
   The empty bleachers roared,

the shadow umpire swept home plate with
   a wisp of wind. Then
Pocoangelini took a
cut and hit one! It was red. As it rose
   over the wall, they roared!

Pocoangelini 38

"You have many wrinkles,"
Pocoangelini told the mirror.
But my wrinkles are of glass, the mirror
replied. "And your hands, Mr. Glass, look like
the talons of a bird."

That is true, the mirror
said, *but my hands **are** made of glass*. It smiled
at Pocoangelini. "Yet glass can
wither too," Pocoangelini said.
"My heart is a glass heart:

"in it a crystal world
spins out its hours in little figures. Snow
falls when one tilts it. Bright fish swim among
coral clouds. Glass can wither," Poco said.
"My heart is a glass heart."

The Door

There is a door
    made of faces
faces snakes and green moss

    which to enter is
        death or perhaps
life which to touch is

    to sense beyond the
        figures carved in
shades of flesh and emerald

    the Inhabitant at home
        in his dark
rooms his hours shadowed or

    lamptouched and that door
        must not be
attempted the moss disturbed nor

    the coiling lichen approached
        because once opened
the visitor must remain in

that place among the
      Inhabitant's couches and
violets must be that man

  in his house cohabiting
    with the dark
wife her daughter or both.

The Attic

Things, the work of dust and summer flies, upstairs over the
   other rooms, lying where they were created under the covers
   of trunks. The mathoms, original art of shadows drowsing in
   boxes: dresses and shirts worn by the seasons at their balls
   and weddings; the toys mice play with; mirrors reflecting
   upon solitude; cords and scissors.

Downstairs the Inhabitant moves slowly among orderly rooms; his
   wife is a comfort, his child little trouble, and the cat is
   kindly for the most part.

In the attic it is quiet; rain touches the roof and falls slowly
   from the eaves.

If the Inhabitant intrudes at odd times he does not notice the
   machine amid the clutter. It stands in a corner behind a
   rack of clothes in shades of brown and yellow, a red flower
   printing itself now and again on some fabric fading into
   the slanted beams.

He is mildly surprised by the numbers of mathoms. At times it
   is hard to remember: a photo in a gilt frame, a ribbon,
   someone's scroll.

They are worth an hour's musing in semidarkness, the hum of a wasp on the ceiling, street sounds muffled. The machine is never discovered: the only mechanism to intrude—lightly, nearly beneath any threshold—is a mower in the hands of a distant neighbor.

When the door of the mathom shop is closed and the Inhabitant leaves the print of his footsteps for a moment on the wooden stair, things pause. There is no movement, not even of time. The mathoms listen until, downstairs, carpets and rugs swallow the noises of living, until the furniture absorbs motion.

Then the machine clicks on: the clock dial begins to turn; dust feeds the cogs. It is making things, making them slowly, out of the debris of afternoons and the streetlamp suicides of evening moths.

It takes forever, but the mathoms accumulate, sift into the corners like drifts, send up an aroma as of the slowest burning—the scent of must. Under the mathom shop the Inhabitant senses—at most, perhaps—a vague weightlessness overhead and, now and then, the cat acts strangely.

The Photograph

It is unwise
to trap a moment such as this
in a frame gilt or
otherwise for such moments

change at any
rate no trap is strong enough look
she lay ensnared in her
layers of clothing among

utter shades here
in this trunk where nothing has influenced
her but clear glass yet
she has grown older

than old her
youth in its fanciful bows shocks the
memory of grays and wrinkles
this creature is absurd

can never have
existed not in any light of any
day under the sun no
one ever lived in

any time so
antique so suffused with ivory and lavender
the odor of bayberry no
camera was ever as

clearly misty no
lens so oval she inhabits an egg
under glass clearly she is
unborn her maturity a

trap for her
discoverer who falls in love with neverness
from which there is no
escape now that she

has been thus
exhumed he will live with her sharing
guilt now and despair forever
in odd moments peering

through crystal into
laces and shadow the long age of
attics hearing only the hornet's
drone and impossible songs.

The Kitchen

In the kitchen the dishwasher is eating the dishes. The Inhabitant listens to the current of digestion—porcelain being ground, silver wearing thin, the hum and bite of the machine.

His wife does not hear it—she is humming, not listening. But the Inhabitant is aware of movement in the cupboards, of the veriest motion—the castiron skillet undergoing metamorphosis, perhaps, becoming its name: the wives' *spider* spinning beneath the counter, weaving and managing, waiting for the doors to open.

Each cup has its voice, each saucer its ear, and the thin chant planes between the shelves, touching the timbres of glass and crystal as it passes. The gentleman listens, is touched to the bone by this plainsong—he feels his response in the marrow's keening.

But the women do not—neither the elder nor the child—sense the music their things make. Their lips move, a column of air rises like steam, and there is something in a minor key sliding along the wall, touching the face of a plastic clock, disturbing the linen calendar beside the condiments.

It is as though, the Inhabitant reflects, the women are spinning. It is as though, while he waits, they weave bindings among the rooms; as though the strands of tune were elements of a sisterhood of dishes, the ladies, the spider in the cabinet, even of the dishwasher, done now with its grinding, which contributes a new sound—a continuo of satiety—to the gray motet the kitchen is singing.

The Cat

Long-haired and black as shadow
the cat comes to drive
a pad of yellow foolscap
and a ballpoint pen out

of the Inhabitant's hands for
it is time again to
handle the palpable dark not
to compose to write about

the loom and shuttle of
shadow moving mechanically across clock
faces but to pass hands
lightly down the pelt of

smooth moments look you no
harm is meant by this
passage it is just that
things were meant to be

this way the waiting the
soft animal with sharp teeth
and claws sheathed lurking in
corners will come out to

be stroked and enjoyed for
it is lethal but sensual
as well and it means
no particular ill the hour

for striking has not arrived
it is not the enemy
but a familiar of houses
a domestic that keeps accounts.

The Scythe

The crescent blade with its snake
  snath hangs on the cellar
    wall waiting for another
      day like last
        summer's milkweed
        day

When the bees in the great patch
  of blossoms out back made
    an electric sound as
      the Inhabitant came
        out to
        whittle

the congregation of stalks into
  a large circle then slowly
    a smaller one scything
      in spirals the
        bees moving
        always

toward the center as the ring
  of petal and stamen contracted
    the stalks falling bleeding
      milk as the
        crescent edge
        stroked

in passing and the buzzing thickened
      at heart until only a
         last fist of milkweed
            stood crowned with
               bees drinking
                  one

nightcap of nectar before dusk cut
      into the still green air
         and the Inhabitant leaned
            on the snath
               against his
                  blade.

Epistles

*I am writing you
from a pit. It is quite dark
here. I see little.
I am scratching this note on a stone.
Where are you? It has been long.*

Thank you for your note.
I do not know where I am.
I believe I may
be with you. It is not dark
here. The light has blinded me.

Death

Who may withstand them,
the dark Rider and the Rose?
On the blue river
a dragon ship sails under
stallion, Rider, and white Rose.

Who must go with them,
the dark Rider and the Rose?
Ancient and infant,
Bishop and maiden await
the black banner of the Rose.

Where will they journey,
the dark Rider and the Rose?
Between two towers
the sun shines. A white stallion
carries riders to the Rose.

American Still Lifes

Hunting Moon

Snow nearly hard as hail
rustles through the bare branches
and settles among the leaves

at the roots of the forest.
In its den of earth
a bear dreams of berries,

of fish gleaming in the shallows.
A herd of deer
shifts edgily in a clearing,

the young bucks shivering.
From a distance
a jay cries

across the gray air.
They are in the wood,
the band of men,

downwind and quiet.
The wind begins to rise.
The snow starts to flake and drift.

The Colony

Rising out of the summer woods
there is a column of smoke
beginning to fade into the sky where,
now and then, a tern or oriole

stitches stillness with a call
and emptiness with a curve of plumage.
The palisade stands open.
The living quarters yawn shadow

into the heat. The fires are cold,
their ash white and fine as snow
on the bare places in the grass.
The blacksmith's tongs lie where they were left;

a water barrel has rolled,
dry as the August wind,
into a corner of the compound.
The woods stand close,

but in them there is no echo—
only the needle rustle of the pines.
The bark on the log paling

has not begun to show moss,
but one of the chief trees or posts
at the right side of the entrance
has the bark taken off,

and five feet from the ground
in fair capital letters is graven
CROATOAN without any cross
or sign of distress.

The Maple Works

In the maple grove wind moves
and the snow grows heavy with water
in the footprints that approach the trunks

where, in each, a box cut collects the sap
that rises to the tap and seeps
heavily into a slat pail.

Over the forest an overcast lowers
and spreads east toward the sea.
The sound of an axe blade chips

at the solid hours filling the spaces
between bole and bole: each cut
is clear and a long way off.

If anything moves it is a naked branch,
its twigs scratching the wind or another limb,
creaking as though a door were opening

or closing between two places, each
unfamiliar and empty, isolate.
In the snow there is fire:

its heat races beneath a tripod
to lick the belly of copper swung there,
filled with the life that rose out of rock

and rises still, vaporous, to fill the grove
with a sweet scent, the steam
lifting past the stirring rod shaped

like an oar and propped against silence,
into the bleak sky blowing overhead
out of the unknown toward the forsaken.

The Meetinghouse

God is kept in this box of pine
beside the road of beaten earth.
A fence of stone holds off the new fields
thinly bitten by the share.

A crow on the limb of a hackmatack
hears his bleak word swallowed by the woods.
The wind from the east, carrying salt,
feels for chinks between the butted boards.

The altar is of oak, as is the table
that raises a pewter goblet to its Host.
Hard benches rest on a bare floor.

Sunlight as spare as the foliage of fall
descends through leaded glass,
illuminates the stillness of an hour
suspended beneath these beams that show their hewing,

beneath the roof that cannot vault,
but peaks and slopes under gray heaven.
The raven calls again, as old as dust,
spreads its shadow climbing through the air,

disappears between a gust and a breath.
The meadow grasses bend. A spate of rain
spatters the fence. A horse
whickers somewhere behind a screen of elms.

The Tavern

The path that passes is of mud.
Rain rattles over the rooftree,
and the wind rustles like a broom.

From the casks at the wall
there rise the scents of hops and apples.
Tables of rough wood and benches of wood

are staggered over the pine floor.
Through the gray windows the sky
lumbers over the forest and downlands,

scatters its March waters among
snow pockets and old furrows.
Now and then, as it passes over

the meetinghouse down the road,
the gale seems to catch a note of hymn
and bring it close. A stack

of fagots on the stone hearth
looks like bone in the shadows
standing at the mouth of darkness.

The Trading Post

Out of the weather, in the first room,
there are knives, blades lying on shelves.
The glinting lamplight slices shadow.

The river passing over the stones of the valley
does not quench with its voices
the flame on the hearth nor the dark fire
of the beads looping the pegs of the wall.

Beyond the logs of the building and its fire
are the boles of the forest bearing firs,
leaves and needles green and sere,
drinking the sun or the sounds of footfall,
light and leather.

In the second room there is a pallet
of pelts and sticks; a musket
lies beside it, its iron rusting.

The air is drowsy with musk and leather—the animals lie
flat or curl in bales
as though listening to the river, or the fire
among the beads and knives,
steel jaws and powder horns.

But the forest lies waking
beyond this frame of logs hewn
in the clearing against the river.
The animals wake listening
for fire and knives and the dark weather.

The Fort

Was it the sound a blue spruce makes
in the wind at night, owls huge
among its needles—

or was it the echo of a footfall
springing among wet leaves and cedar boughs
on the riverbank? A light foot

in deer leathers, and the moon
lying like a quicksilver crosscurrent
on the water. The ghost-holes

of the fort on the point
make square spaces out of shadow, and the dark
bores of muskets forged of rust

aim into the sibilant wood.
There are fissures in the night,
dark eyes waking, time seeping

through the oak limbs and the maple limbs.
All the tribe shall gather
to make war paint out of the river

and its roots, their lips saying over and over,
it is time for war—let the children
and women take cover

in the pine copses while the men
storm shadow, while the fusillade
storms about them out of the stockade

like so many windows, and their arrows answer
as if the shafts were night birds
calling from spruce to spruce.

The Pharmacy

The odor is of sulphur and autumn.
On the high bench at the back
there are pipettes and flasks,
a wooden mortar with its worn pestle,
alchemical spoons.

In the counter there are grooves
for rolling pills, a broken pill or two,
some powder, and honey in a jug.
On the shelves are tinted bottles
like gothic spires in small:

simples and decoctions,
extracts and infusions,
tinctures ink-labeled.
In drawers and bins pomander balls
roll out their round scents.

Ointments stand tinned
beside electuaries boxed,
and from the beams there depend
the sere leaves of lupine,
Indian root and lavender.

It is quiet among the cures.
The rumble of a cartwheel on the street
mutters barely through the door
to disturb oxeye at blind gaze,
the ills of the world at bay.

The College

The wall is of brick. The buildings
are brick. Red brick flags underfoot.
Within these hallowed precincts
all is just, Divine.

The trees turn over a new leaf,
then another. They are rooted
in thin soil. Their shade
stubbles the grass, stipples cobbles.

Outside the compound drays
carry hay from the manger
to the town stable. A bell
peals the hour out of heaven.

A candle sheds small light
on the Word in a dusky room.
The portrait on the wall is robed,
its periwig haloing a hard stare.

Candles glow in the grate.
The shelves speak volumes:
the fatted calf has been slain
in order to bind them to order.

There shall be commerce
between earth and Heaven—
the steeple aspires over the cobbles,
ringing the changes on bell, brick, and candle.

The Courthouse

The legal arm has reached up from the sea
along the estuary, past the straits
and narrows, negotiated rapids till
it has banked upon this plot among the pines.

The panes stare blindly at the dawn
that breaks across the bar, spills to the floor,
begins to ease enlightenment
upwards of the stairwell and the rail.

In the living quarters there are books,
calfbound, upon the shelf.
The day's eye, falling through bull's-eye glass,
picks out in gilt the letters of the law.

The Ferry

The cable bows downward,
touches the surface at midstream,
then curves to the far bank—

there, all is the same: the same woods
receding from the dock, squeezing the gravel track
to a certain point under the horizon.

The river is in flood, the water muddy.
Under the pier the pilings are in jeopardy.
Carp hug the eddy bottoms.

The barge pulls at its ties, strains the cable
running through eyes along the gunwale.
A smoky crane blows downstream

against its will, tacking westward
like the eroding light.
To the east dusk is breaking

along the road, submerging the forest,
touching toward a clearing where light
swims in a window, washes

into the dooryard: a pump, a trough,
a stack of wood, an axe,
its head glinting in a cleft.

The cable hums in the gale,
its fibers binding silence to silence.
The bell on the pier utters a note.

When its mate responds on the far crossing
night will fall in cataract,
the halves of earth be sundered and set adrift.

The Tollhouse

The bell rings once and then the woods are still.
Something startles and rustles in the shed.
In the dooryard the pump has not been primed.
The axe stands rusting in its cleft.

The mortar in the chimney turns to lime.
The fence is down beside the meadow;
nearby an apple tree stands knotted,
a woodchuck hole opening in its root.

A catbird in gray patrols the field
from limb to stump to lilac bush in bloom.
The wooden plow bleaches in a patch
of herbs and weeds: alumroot

and larkspur, thistle, trailing vetch.
The sun is warm and curling, warping shake
and shingle, the cord of peeling wood
that musts to lichen near the gate.

Toadstools like coins are spent beneath the elm.
The window glass is dusty, dusty webs
travel the breeze and catch in every gust.
The forest ponders at the door.

The road moves west through trees toward the river,
the crossing barge, the pier, toward the sun
beginning now to fall beyond the current.
The bell rings twice and then the woods are still.

The Mill

The mill grinds the night
into dark flours which the river wind
blows among the trees along its bank

like pumice or mist. A coon
or some other animal stirs darkness
into leaves and underbrush

as it burrows along the mill wall.
The stream, cascading down from its pitch
and fall, turns the night sounds

like a great wheel, drowns the moon
in turbulence. It rises there, the building,
between those pine tips that spear midnight

in the gully—rises and disappears
and reappears as the villagers,
in mufflers and shawls, come in a long line

for sacks of umbra to make their bread.
The line wavers along the stream bed down
almost to the river. Their hands,

extended out of frost,
accept the starlight. They turn to walk
back to town and home,

for they have shadow now to sustain shadow.
And as the wind comes up it blows them to earth—
blows the mill itself into mist, all

but the great stone
which rolls into the lichen and fern
along the stream to be still until tomorrow.

The Ice House

The walls are of rough plank.
Time melts slowly in the straw
without reflection—
it is like dwale in glass.
A pole with a hook hangs from a spike.

In the room where the saws are kept
silence is finely honed.
Beneath the floor it is damp and cool.
The still lives of the riverbank,
summer-hunted, burrow there.

Upstream an eagle sweeps the river;
a trumpet vine snows into a gully.
A boat, frozen against the current,
lies near the field where a sledge
turns its runners into loam.

Summer seeps toward falls
recollected in eddies along the brink.
The hazes of August turn to mist
when the door is opened and closed
where winter is in keeping.

The Ropewalk

The building is a telescope of wood,
the sea a glittering eye looking from the east
through dusk toward the hills.

Before the open door at either end
a stanchion rises, a great rope
spun and wound about, between.

Beside the wharves the vessels
lie among the screels of gulls.
The rope is undone; its splayed end
lies where it was laid upon the boards.
Bales of hemp are stacked along the walls.

Light falls backward through the scents
of salt and fiber.
Stillness ravels as the tide
siles along the keel, beside the hull.

The sun rolls down the rocks above the shore:
the flare of flint and steel,
and in the dark the coiling fuse of time.

The Schooner

Even as she slides down the ways
alga begins to green her planks.
Sunlight strikes through the early haze
into the gray-blue water.
There are gulls, and a ruffled pelican
perched on a bollard.
In the bay there are shapes
tremulous among groves of weed and seagrass.

Rust begins to take the anchor
and climb the chain.
The canvas seems cloudy;
the sun's edges fray on the deck.
In the fissures of a ledge anemones bloom.

There is smoke on the horizon
as she moves toward open water,
and as she passes fields and pastures
the plowing stops,
the horses sag in their traces,
the white houses begin yellowing like fall.

The House

Upstairs there is a bed
among the spiders and the moonlit chairs,
the loveseats made of shadow.

The book on the table has leaves
brown as the elm's.
Its cover is of moss.

A pair of trousers blows in the draft
as though the legs were filled
with nothing more than webs.

Tables, spindle-legged, stand in the corners.
The carpets are worn to threads.
In at the window the owl asks and asks,
and the swift answers from the chimney.

The Silo

Two great elms. Hills beyond them;
fields and a white hillhouse.
Windrows filled with snow,
the rest, hay stubble.
Silence rustles along the road.

The trees are set to snarl the air just so,
their limbs stark in the morning,
and in them the redbird rouses.

Through the mist of limbs
there is a silo with its gray barn:
a swallow climbs up the still air
with straw in its beak,
and another dives down
through the haze and a flock of sparrows.

In the hills there are feldspar and quartz,
colors dull as the leaves the wind has used.
The clouds, white as whey,
skim the firs, small animals
concerned with windfalls,
and the hawk in the spiral currents.

The Covered Bridge

The snow is thin and wet
under the early winter clouds.
The wind has fallen.
The river is gray in reflection.

Only one horse-and-wagon has passed
along the road since dawn:
the hoofprints are small wells,
and the wheel tracks follow like canals—

they stop at the bridge, at the sill
flush with the brink. The roof
interposes shadow and gingerbread
between heaven and rapids.

There is the chance of echo for a space,
bare boards, a suspension.
Morning looks into the passage.
On the other side the tracks begin again.

The Tobacco Shed

September comes smoking over the hills
to lie on the fields smoldering.
Dust puffs among dry stalks and weeds.
The sun is old fire upon the clouds.

In the shed August hangs
sere and golden,
leaves browning among the slatted walls.
Shadow is thick in the heavy air.

Swallows sew the murk among the beams:
leaves and feathers, chittering and veins,
the harvest waiting to be consumed
in the waiting clay, waiting

to be snuffed like August, September,
like the lamps in the drawing rooms
or on the masts of the ships at anchor,
like the candles in the shanties in the pinewoods.

The Stable

The morning in the windows smells blue.
Over the great door a horseshoe has been nailed,
its open end up so its luck won't run out.
There is straw in the stalls.

The nails have rusted;
one has broken, and the shoe tilts.
Boards have been slatted across
the panes of some windows.

Dew mists off the lawns and meadows,
clover and ivy.
There are thunderheads to the south,
cold gusts out of the north.

Somewhere the roans and grays are running,
early sunlight turning the dust saffron,
alfalfa and cotton forgotten for the race—

but not here where harness flakes
against the planks, the pitchfork
grows splinter-brittle;
not here where the morning blurs
and runs to sable in the spider's corner.

The Depot

The rails pause barely to tie the horizons
where the wheat fields curve into day and night.
A wooden cart, long-handled and iron-wheeled,
stands in shadow under the baggage sign.
Dust settles in the road on the other side.

The great hand hides the small
on the face of the town hall tower.
Behind the ticket window grill
there is small disagreement:
the railroad's time depends and seldom falters.

A valise lies on the green bench
upon the platform:
the planks show their weathers.
A cicada buzzes in a cindered elm.
The door blisters and stands ajar.

A hawk whose shadow crosses the tracks
can see the pigeon's lighter gray
against the slate, the iron flue.
The dirt track follows the rails,
then turns north among the fields.

Houses diminish; now and then
a silo pierces the yellows and rusts.
There may be a thunderhead
somewhere at the edge of things.
There may be smoke and a thin sound.

The Trestle

The rails shine like new wire
in the moonlight; the beams and girders
are a fretwork holding the hills.
The gorge holds darkness in cascade.

If a whistle lies like an echo
upon the prairie, among the stones
of the rising ground, it is perhaps an owl
or a coyote among the pines.

The wind hums in the frame.
A rock clicks and splashes,
sharp as silence in the starlight.
Something touches the tall grass

and curves again into the air.
On the high bluff a hump shifts,
then another and another—

the rails begin to sing in the wind;
there is a lowing; there are sparks
among the stars. Then the earth moves:
it is a dune of shadow

that makes the trestle shudder,
that fills the gorge
with the sound of avalanche,
hair, horn, bone, and blood.

The Homestead

In the morning there is the east wind
carrying dust the color
of a darker sun
past the silo and the cribs.

At dead noon there is a pause.
The land bakes into its ruts and rows.

Then again the wind blows,
now from the west, taking soil back
over the cupola with its rusting cock,
past the screen porch, its door swinging.
The horned toads clamber into rock.

In the evening the house settles
down into the red dark.
The plains and fields crool
beneath the windows' oblongs of light.

When even the echoes of echoes cease,
beneath sensation
there is a strange sound
like wet things sliding:
the ghost of a comber, a slimming off,
then again a comber.

From far back and down deep
there is the scent of salt
and a falling off from the silent edge.

The Stockyard

The lake that looks like a sea
fades into the descending sky:
there is no horizon.
It is just dawn.
The city smokes into the clouds.

In the snags of the pens' rails
tufts of hair bristle at morning.
The earth is pitted, partly ice, partly dung.
It is difficult to discern shapes
except for breath like fog
rising out of the darkness.

The rails make oblongs and oblongs.
Somewhere a bell wakens
among the sheds and alleys, along the streets.
Upon the ramps there is a memory
of slow passage; there are mallets
that stand, heads down, on floors
the color of rust.

The Observation Tower

It has a black throat,
iron stairs ascending.
The stars scatter above the park below:
the mirror lake is a tarn
swallowing night.
The air is edgy and warm.

In a car stopped among the trees
a radio plays the blues.
The tower breathes a vapor
of perfume and planets.
The wind gusts, and there is a scent
of damp stone rising.

The rock face falls away from the brink
into maple and elm.
Along the road in the near distance
streetlamps and nighthawks descend toward town.
To the east the hills break,
and beyond them is the sea combing sand.

The Church

In the basement it is cool
among the tables, the small chairs,
the folding screens and crayons.
The lavatory is damp, the water runs;
there is room for webs and fables.

The wooden stair ascends and turns
into heat settled among the pews.
The altar rises above the golden oak
which dark juice has stained.
Frayed wine runs down the center aisle
away from the electric keys,
the hymnals with the broken covers.

Summer lies upon the step before the door,
beneath the white clapboards,
the pictures peeling from the glass.
The gate of pipe and wire stands ajar.

Next door the parsonage is scaled to dolls.
It takes the corner,
facing another neighborhood.
Six garages stand by a gravel drive.
A pear tree withers there, and on the curb
an elm like a cathedral stays alive.

The Barn

Behind the locked doors
swallows stitch shadow to make
a sampler of perpetual dusk.
Summer's hull tilts against the wall.

A gray car looms into rust,
its doors closed against silence.
A rain of motes slants to fall
upon an iron stove cast in hay.

Wind leans through the window
from the fields beyond where,
dimmed by the spider's cataract,
sunlight wanes into goldenrod.

The stumps of the two great elms
have colored themselves in the barn's reflection.
The road passes.
Under the bank the brown river ebbs.

A Cage of Creatures

& *A Maze of Monsters*

Dybbuk

It is in her eyes—the odd light,
and behind it a shadow, as though
        someone were masked and helpless,
        held captive and speechless. She moves

        tautly. It is as if her flesh
were not her own: The muscles lag so
        briefly one is hardly sure
        they lag at all. The lips are hard

        as agate; the cheeks are pallid;
the eyes hollow and blue. When she laughs,
        the sound comes from far away,
        sharp as an echo from a ledge.

The people in the room raise their
glasses and drink, uneasy at her
        approach. They cannot hold her
        gaze—the men shuffle, catch themselves;

        the women smile like wire, for
there is no way to help. One must save
        oneself first, furtively. One
        must skime her from under lowered

lids, judge her intentions, and then,
without being obvious, when she
        turns her head, move away. We
        know of her possession by that

        dead thing. What is one to do? Too
late, it is too late. Bad enough when
        we are at home undressing
        afterward, to chance to glimpse in

        the glass the unfamiliar form
of someone we nearly recognize—
        to startle; to stare until
        shape and features some clear at last

        and we can swallow the pulse that
has leapt into the throat, raise a hand
        awkwardly to smooth the hair,
        brittle as wire, along the bone.

Fetch

To step out of a bedroom
into a forest of darkness;
to find oneself naked among brambles
and shagbark, a low wind making the flesh rise.
To turn and discover there is no door,
only bellbloom and shadow.

And this is waking, the path
beaten hard beneath heaven, stars
among limbs bare of season. And between
trees, glass—dark sheets parsing silence without
image. In the wood only the mutter
and crool of water wending.

Pause and touch: Merely surface
smooth and cold among the boles. Search:
Only the ghost of reflection paling
under gaze. Walk, cover the ground. Know there is
neither graith nor tackle to take the wood.
Move as through one more tunnel.

Stop when you feel him near. Strain
to see who stands in the way, who
holds out his hand, loof and hardel: It is
another mirror of the wood—no: Likeness
of quicksilver. Behind him, a bedroom
lies rumpled in a gilt frame.

It is dark, but he is known.
He is the beast of whom they have
spoken so often in living rooms and
dreams. It is a familiar forest. This is
one's own path. It is the Fetch beckoning
welcome to the crystal glade.

Grendel

In the lowlands lie his reaches,
in the salt-queaches. Fogs and fens
he inhabits. Horrid by day
deep in his delvings where he sleeps
hard by his mother, by moongleam
he is *most* monstrous, *most* ugsome.
Night's eye closes as he clointers,
shambling through shallows to find food—
this scaly fiend, this feared foeman,
eater of carls, doomed damerel,
great gunsel. Why do his hungers
cause him to clamber from the deeps,
the tide's womb, to forbidden flesh,
the meat of men? It is not meet
he should hound us in the meadhall
under the alecask as we neeze
fleering in dream, noddles bobbing.
We whommle and wake—ah! the wight
has us in hand! The cumberworld
slobbers and slavers. Snithe his breath
upon our napes! His fingers prog;
his fangs are fastles on our flesh—
then home to mother through the mirk,
to the dark dens at the deep's verge,
there to drowse while the daylight lies
on barrow and beach and gull-buoy.

Homunculus

"Thank you," it said when she uncovered it,
having drawn the curtains, made sure the door was locked.
"I was beginning to think you had forgotten me."
It smiled, blinking in the electric light.

She sighed, began to fix a meal.
It watched as she worked slowly, gathering the few
utensils, heating the food. When she sat down it said,
"This smells good." It sniffed. It was awkward

for her to bend over the plate.
Through the door she could see the photographs upon
the wall of the other room: The dead man and the child
become an adult she rarely saw.

When she was through she washed the things.
"Please don't splash," it said. Afterward she could relax
and watch her evening show. She caught herself glancing to
the phone sometimes. "I don't think it will

"ring," it said; it was right, of course.
Outdoors the traffic faded; the lamps came on in
windows, on the streets. "It's time for bed," it told her when
the city lay stupored in its mist.

She rose, turned out the light so that
she would not have to see the body with its veins,
the sagging breasts, the gut—and sprouting out of it, the
little man, perfect as a child, grown

nearly out of her by now, as
the other one had done so long ago.

Juggernaut

Grandfather of mammoths,
ancestor of wool and ivory,
 he contained the grasslands
 that might not contain him.

Pillars of cypresswood
bore up a mount that might itself have
 borne up a ziggurat
 beside the river's draught.

What strength was in his loins,
lustihood in his navel—gristle
 like iron plates, like pipes
 of bronze his body's bones!

Lakes have formed in his prints,
as the fisherfolk well remember.
 He has gone to the reeds
 which are thin and many.

Leviathan

Morning touches the waves and breaks
over the whitecaps where the ship cuts
through the waters turning an early blue.
The wind is fresh in the east.
Spume rinses the deck now and again.

The light strengthens as the sun rides
a high scud in rising flight.
Nothing moves to the horizon beyond
susurruses of the sea.
The ship rolls, and as she rolls she waits.

Then sunlight touches a fountain
rising from ocean abeam.
The ship shudders into pursuit at flank.
A sharp sound shatters the wind.
A coil of line unwinds, following

its shaft over the combers. Stain
tints the fluid of a wave,
and a great fluke rises into the air,
then falls in an explosion
of froth—Leviathan goes sounding.

The shallower waters glitter;
with depth, they begin to dim.
Farther down, in the fathoms, there is night
perpetual and cold; there
is darkness rising breathless and deep.

Minotaur

In my dream there is light
in the underground passage
turning between stone block walls.
The floor is a shallow stream.

How have I come to be
here in this place with my son,
not yet a yearling? Danger
waits nearby—one can feel it.

He must be preserved. At
the end of the passage there
is safety—another thing
I know, but cannot tell how.

The water moves slowly,
but it can bear him in this
frail shell in which I place him.
And he has been set afloat.

As he drifts through stone, through
light, he rises, leans upon
the rim to fathom water.
It is true: Pain is depthless.

My feet move to follow,
to seat my child again, but
the fluid drags at my flesh.
I call; he does not look back.

As he diminishes
in the curve of his passage,
I sense the beast I have feared
in the distance between us.

Nasnas

It must hop, having but one leg,
    but it does so swiftly.
    They say its flesh is sweet.
    It can give half a smile,
    but its laugh is grotesque,

so Nasnas snirtles instead, to
    keep its mouth as close as
    may be; thus, it tries to
    suppress its yawn as well.
    If it winks with one eye,

it is blind a moment and may
    be captured then. If one
    listens at its breast, to
    the half-beat of the heart's
    single chamber, one hears,

besides, the lone lung's suspiring.
    Its nostril flares in half-
    hearted anger. It can
    give but partial comfort.
    God knows how it makes love.

Odradek

At first one might take it
merely for another mathom:
a useless treasure such as may be found
in a littered attic or lost
within a dim closet, toward the back—

star-shaped, made of sticks, wrapped
in thread-ends, knotted and tangled,
of many textures, thicknesses, colors.
There is a small crossbar of wood
glued by an end to the star's center, and

held to the rod, at right
angles, another rod—a leg
on which, together with a starpoint, it
stands upright. If you address it
on the stairs where often it lurks, it will

tell its name, the tattered
threads trembling, and then laugh like dry
leaves rustling. Look for Odradek and it
will be absent for as long as
you remember. But in the fall, perhaps,

a solemn wind wrapping
    the eaves, you will climb dusty stairs
into the garret, looking for—you know
    not what: A sheet of paper, sere
at the edges, on which your father wrote;

    a clock with a painted
    face, time run out of it. And there,
behind a chest, near the dry carcass of
    a moth, a fly, Odradek will
stand raveling. You will ask, "Where have you

    "been?" But it will stand mute,
    spindling silence, draggling shadow.
You will shrug at last in the chill, droning
    afternoon, begin to rummage.
When you look up, Odradek will have gone.

Roc

Stones are falling from the sky
somewhere at sea. The clouds part,
and a boulder edges through, slowly,
froths of vapor trailing from its edges.

As it descends, behind it
there is another, and yet
another: A column of stones
dropping toward the cool blue mere below.

They have always been falling,
for how else would there be waves?
The brown surface of a stone touches
the water, dimples it; a circle swells

about its bulk like the lips
of surprise. The mouth swallows.
The astonished wave widens, begins
to roll toward the islands and the coast.

It picks up substance and size,
the fluid force moving through—
not made of—water, this strength of stone.
Within the zero zone another grows.

No one knows where the boulders
    fall to sea; no one has seen
  the bird, great beak filled with rocks, the cairn
of time piling upon the lost sea bed.

Sasquatch

with apologies to John Ciardi

After the wind-tempest, when
branches lie in crambles upon the clearings
and neighbors at far distances phone
down the foothills under the mountains

to ask if all is well still,
the answer is "Yes" and, sometimes, "But have you
seen anything of a shambling man
dressed in furs running before the birds'

"chirming just before the sun
was wiped out of the slate sky and the rain erased
the trees, made them slop and wiggle like
pines in a fingerpainting?" And, "No,"

is the answer, "not this time,
but now you mention it, last time we thought we
saw a bear at the edge of the woods,
and when we went to look there were prints

"in the mud—footprints the shape
of a big man's, a huge man's bare feet. They put us
in mind of the manse of the films,
the girl in the chiffon gown walking

"down the hall to stop under
a portrait whose eyes move. And then, you know, it
    slides aside, and a hairy arm comes
    reaching out toward the maiden, and

    "we scream, don't we, for the girl
in the white gown, but you know, what must it be
    like to be the thing the arm belongs
    to? What wouldn't we want, and wouldn't

    "we hide in the walls and woods?
And if a storm blew up, wouldn't we wander some,
    down from the timberline to where the
    houses started, to look in windows

    "at firelight and carpets,
to think about chiffon and wish the folk would
    understand somehow, somewhen, that there's
    a bit of hairy arm in everyone?"

Werewind

When she died she became a wind.
Her body turned to dust, but her breath
expanded to fill the landscape of her mind
and to inhabit an old geography:
the hills and plains of childhood and the vales
of her despair. She looked down

out of the cloudy air to see
the house she had abandoned filling
with life again. She blew out of the maples,
eased to the windows, tried to filter under
the sash to breathe through the familiar rooms.
This she was denied, but when

the children issued from the doors
to play in the yard she bent the grass
before them, chilled their toes, whispered they were not
welcome in the place where she had never felt
anything but a stranger, and stranger
still in her body of air.

Although they paused to listen, though
they thought a voice was speaking to them
that they recognized from dreams from which they woke
with a vague sorrow born of midnight shadow,
they soon were taken with another thought,
or an image from the bright

world there before them. And at last,
grown weary even of couching in
the roots of nightshade, listening to the sounds
of ordinary passages of bone and blood,
she traveled north, moving against the grain
of the autumn flocks, seeking

the climes and means of flesh. She came
where she belonged by temperament at
last. She recognized as part of her the floes
and washes of her life, the life she had made
out of thin air, and there she would remain,
feeding on herself and on

the white bones of the winter of her despair.

Xoanon

        Its body is like that
of a buffalo, black and thick.
        It is lugsome as mud.
It depresses me to think of it,
        lying there in the corner
under a table of my study.

        It is best that I not
look at it, though its eyes are closed.
        I have fed it a root
of nightshade, and it is sleeping. It
        will not cast me one of its
killing glances for a while. It is

        content in its despair.
Its dreams fill that boar skull and spill
        out of the bristles, rank
as gorge, into lamplight. I try not
        to watch these visions in shades
of pallor and nocolor. Its neck

        querls about its body,
translucent as intestine. In
        it, slowly spiraling,
the nightshade darkens and dissolves. If
        I rise, it will rise as well.
Its lids will open to slits, its neck

uncoil; it will lumber
after me, nearly stepping on
        its chin, for I have tamed
Xoanon. I stop and stare it down.
        It moans, heaves beneath my bed
to watch me dream of it. The beast knows

        its master, knows that I
will not think of it if I will,
        that I can strike to its
heart with a look. And Xoanon knows
        as well parasite from host,
knows who shall cast the last glance at last—

who is the master's *bete noir.*

Zombie

Outside the door, the noises of the sleugh.
Indoors, the tropic heat, the potted ferns,
a palm stuck in the corner near the couch.
She waits and picks at lint. Her fingers run
through her hair. "It's nerves, just nerves," she says,
but still she listens.
                        And then the sudden knock.
The potted palm sweats. Its leaves ripple.
She cannot speak. Then—"Yes, who is it?" She
gets up and smooths her skirt. Another knock.

She goes toward the door. The mirror there
beside the clock shows her what she must see:
a plain young woman with faded eyes, her hair
a neutral shade. "What does he want with me?"
she tells the glass.
                        "Who's there?" she asks again.
"I've come," he says. She reaches for the knob.
Her palms are sweating: they slip as her fingers turn.
She pauses—pulls.
                        He stands there on the stoop,
his eyes too bright and blank. His puffy skin
is white as mallow in the dimming light.
He has no hair. His body is too stiff.
His mouth gapes as he looks at her. She starts,
but catches herself. His hat is in one hand;
the other goes to his tie. He clears his throat.

142

"We'd better hurry," she says, "or we'll be late."
She turns off the light, picks up her coat, her purse,
and moves toward the door. He stands aside,
closes the door, and follows her into the night.

FROM

The Compleat Melancholick

The Menu of Melancholy

Out of Burton's *The Anatomy of Melancholy*

These do generally ingender gross humours
  and windy bile, fill "all those inward parts
 with obstructions: Beef, goat's flesh (a filthy beast,
and rammish); hart & red deer hath an evil name,
  it yields gross nutriment, next unto horse";

all venison is melancholy, and begets
  bad blood; hare breeds incubus; conies are
 of the like nature; pork "may breed a quartan
ague." All fish are discommended, for they breed
  "viscosities, slimy nutriment, lit-

"tle and humourous nutriment; eel, tench, lamprey,
  crawfish; all fish, that standing pools and lakes
 frequent, yield bad juice and nourishment, dried, soused,
indurate fish, as ling, fumadoes, red herrings,
  sprats, stockfish, haberdine, poor-John; all shell

"fish, conger, sturgeon, turbot, mackerel, skate. Amongst
  fowl, peacocks and pigeons, all fenny fowl
 are forbidden, as ducks, geese, swans, herns, cranes, coots,
didappers, waterhens, with all those teals, curs, shel-
  drakes and peckled fowls." Among herbs: "Gourds, cow-

"cumbers, coleworts, melons, cabbage; all raw herbs and
  sallets breed melancholy blood; roots &

sole food are windy and bad, or troublesome
to the head; as onions, garlick, scallions, turnips,
    carrots, radishes, parsnips. All manner

"of fruits" are forbidden, "as pears, apples, cherries,
        plums, strawberries, nuts, medlers, 'serves, sweetings,
    pearmains, pippins, grapes & figs. All pulse are naught:
beans, pease, fitches, &c."—they fill the brain with gross
        "fumes, breed black thick blood," cause troublous dreams. Of

"spices: Pepper, ginger, cinnamon, cloves, mace, dates,
        honey and sugar; all aromatics,
    all sharp & sour things, luscious & oversweet,
or fat, as oil, vinegar, verjuice, mustard, salt;
        bread of baser grain, as pease, beans, oats, rye,

"or overhard baked, crusty & black, oats and corn.
        All black wines; overhot, compound, strong drinks,
    as Muscadine, Malmsey, Alicant, Rumney,
Brown Bastard, Metheglin, Cyder & Perry. Beer
        overnew or over stale, over strong

"or not sod, that smells of the cask, sharp or sour—
        it frets and galls because of the hop." And
    compound strong dishes beyond these simples: "Puddings
stuffed with blood, baked meats, soused, indurate meats fried &
        broiled; condite; milk, and all that comes of milk,

"—cheese, curds; all cakes, simnels, buns, cracknels, made with
        butter, &c.; fritters, pancakes,
    pies, sausages, & those several sauces, sharp
or oversweet." And waters last: "Standing waters,
        thick & ill-colored, such as come forth of

148

"pools and moats, where hemp hath been steeped or fishes live,
    are most unwholesome, putrefied, full of
  mites, creepers, slimy, muddy, unclean, corrupt,
impure." All are windy, full of melancholy.
    Shun them by dawn and dusk, by dark and light.

Blood Deeper than Night

. . . he is born naked, and falls awhining
at the very first, he is swaddled and bound up
like a prisoner, cannot help himself,
and so he continues to his life's end.
—Pliny, as quoted by Burton.

Where have these strangers come from,
        those who cannot sleep?
    This is the bone of one
and the flesh of another.
    I hold them in my hand
like ivory and velvet.

They are clothed in blood deeper
        than night in the glass.
    They walk about, utter
what I cannot hear. They sink
    and rise. Their substance is
runic—parchment turned to smoke.

They chant in the vein; they tell
        lyrics out of plasm.
    The temple is groined where
they read without light. Under
    the palm they are silent
among their dark alphabets.

When will these strangers walk down
        into my waking?
    This is the word of one,
the silence of another.
    I hold them in my palm
like parchment and ivory.

150

The Moon of Melancholy

. . . a silly country fellow . . . killed
his ass for drinking up the moon,
that he might restore the moon to the world.
—Burton

It was late when they came in
through the gate. He dismounted
beside the water trough, and the donkey
dropped its nose into the moon to drink.

He stood fatigued underneath
the wind scudding high cloud. No
light beyond reflection lit the windows
of the house. The barn soughed. The long grass

of the fields grew longer in
shadow laid over shadow.
The journey had taken forever. For
as long as it takes to remember,

he forgot where he had been,
and then recalled again. He
closed his eyes, listened to the beast drinking,
and was afraid, suspended

in the stillness of his mind.
When he looked again, when wind
had become too hollow against silence,
he found his eyes were opened,

but still he could not see. His
animal had drunk the moon
out of the water. He tried to discern
clouds, moon, sky, stars, the edge of the wind,

but found there a well into
which he felt himself to be
sinking. It was a vortex no world
could withstand. In the morning he wept

over the animal that
had carried him home; he wept
in the sun that had risen with him. He
remembered the image of

bone, restored as the blade sank
homing: The moon floating in
the trough of water and blood, and the wind
not quite too hollow to bear.

The Desert of Melancholy

They have myriads in their mouths.
—Burton

It is not far from here to
nowhere. Merely across the furniture.
We are experiencing
technical difficulties; please

do not adjust. If there were
ink in this pen, it would be different.
However, it is not. This,
then, is a poem written among

furniture, on paper like
a glass screen, pen like a stainless steel steak
knife. It is a poem made of
mirrors. In it you will see, if

you look technically, small
creatures dancing on the head of a pin—
any number of them: I
have myriads in my mouth. They

do not know that they are there—
no more than we know they are watching us.
Well, quite a charming place, this,
wherever: Chairs, tables, the smell

of meat in the air. No one
will wonder at this devastation of
syllables. Who is to be
awed? It is my devastation,

and I am past wonderment.
It is at this point precisely that the
cactus must resume blossom.
If it does not, words will have no

point. Expect nothing. You will
be disappointed in other things. The
desert does not flower.
It is the flower that flowers.

That Particular Air

How come they to dig up fish bones, shells, beams,
iron-works, many fathoms under ground, & anchors
in mountains far remote from all seas?
—Burton

The hook has let go,
and the Conestoga
has rolled down the cliff, along
with the television set. All
the women sorrow,
for their struggle has

been for nothing, which
they have achieved. The men
do not give up. They have yet
to understand that the wagon
train will not get through.
Of course, the wagon

train will not follow
the Tube, it will follow
the script; the prairie schooners
will reach California. There,
the women will gaze
at the Pacific

Ocean; glance, with that
particular air, at
each other, at their men; they
will lie down to have the children
who sit on the shore:

"You owe to yourself
your own destruction."

Winter in Muscovy

*In Muscovy . . . they live in stoves
and hothouses all winter long.*
—Burton

Open any grate, any glass gate
on a street of cast iron or glass,
and someone will say, "Hello," out from between
flames or fronds, white teeth smiling in a soot face:
A flowerchild, an elder or alderman,
a young lady in pince-nez

with a potbelly, tendrils in her
hair—"Hello, come in, enjoy, enjoy
'May-games, Wakes, and Whitsun-Ales!'" All winter long
in their stoves they make feast with "rare devices
to corrivate waters, musick instruments,
& trisyllable Echoes,

"again, again, & again repea-
ted [ted ted] with myriads of such."
But if ye be melancholick, enter not,
nor lay thine eyes longing on these revelers—
"Let them freely feast, sing and dance, have their Puppet-
plays, Hobbyhorses, Tabers,

"Crowds, Bagpipes, play at Ball, and Barley-
breaks—an Index of Ignorance—let
them go as they are in the Catalogue of
Ignoramus, snorting on a bulk," although
"nothing can be more excellent and pleasant,
so abstruse and recondite,

"so bewitching, so miraculous,
   so ravishing, so easy withal
& full of delight" as these baubles of stove-
dwellers, inhabitants of glass houses,
these multifarious "Martian amulets,
         Weapon Salve, Universal

"Balsams, strange extracts, Elixirs of
   Life," 'cause that's not where It's at; let one
take heed he do not overstretch his wits and
         make a skeleton of himself.

Stone and Shadow

. . . . many cannot sleep for Witches and
fascinations, which are too familiar
in some places . . . .
—Burton

It is as still as falling
  in this house of weathers.
Nothing but lamplight and the shadow of my hand
  lie along the page. The clock
    owns everything.

I have been dreaming of the
  woman. She has faces
to burn. The day's fire is black upon the flagging.
  I listen for wind within
    the flue; there is

only the dark sound of coals
  rising to enter night
smoking over the rooftree. Still, the woman is here
  under towels—or standing
    in a wardrobe

among sleeves and lapels.
  I see her eyes clearly
between the strokes of an hour. She is of a size
  and a certain shape. She has
    loved me in time.

Logs lie at the hearth between
    four dark chimes. I would know
her, for it is said, "She sees within the stone beneath
    the shadow." She is shadow.
        And I am stone.

Failed Fathers

On a theme by,
and with apologies to, Greg Pape

     Where do all the failed fathers
go? To Albuquerque? Cleveland?
After the slow slide down the drain,
where do they go? After the last
lay-off, the class reunion where they're shown

     kissing the matronly Queen
of the Prom, where do they go. Where
do they go, these old young men, these
paunchy guys with the eyes that squint
into the lens at the family picnic,

     the fishing expedition
near the falls, the baseball game where
they played second? After the fights,
the money fights, the brief affair,
after the spree and the morning after,

     where do the failed fathers go?
Is there a bar where they gather,
is there a bus they all take,
is there a line at the Bureau
where they talk over their sons and daughters,

their Old Ladies turning cold,
the milkmen they caught spending time
drinking coffee in their kitchens?
Is there a motel in Cleveland
full of fathers playing poker,

smoking cigarettes, squinting
at their hands, drinking beer? Is there,
down in Albuquerque, some street
full of walk-up rooms full of dreams
of mowing lawns, of paneling basements,

propping children on their bikes,
walking down the aisles of markets
pushing shopping carts? Of course, we
know what happens to our mothers,
but where oh where do the failed fathers go?

Farewell to Melancholy

*It is most true, the style proclaims the man, our style
bewrays us, & as hunters find their game by the trace,
so is a man descried by his writings. I have laid myself open
(I know it) in the Treatise, and shall be censured I doubt not,
yet this is some comfort: our censures are as various as our palates.
If I be taxed, exploded by some, I shall happily be as much
approved & commended by others.*
—Burton

If night is staining the window,
let the streetlight take care of it,
    washing it into the road
        with the neighbors' dreams.
It is March, unseasonably warm

    in this garret where my clothes hang
    about my shoulders. Music is
        sneaking out of the books and
            writhing in the last
cactus. The gerbil has died, but I

    hear his wheel looming something in
    and out of shadow. My father,
        whom the mouse has followed, casts
            a hard stare askance
out of his frame. He is young and

    will not forgive me. I can feel
    my words crinkle among his ash.
        The new Christbearer under
            me sleeps; the aging
wife, the pubescent girl. I have looked

into the window and seen what
the streetlamp can do with plain glass,
    quicksilver, the image of
    a human life, with
night and the past stored in beds, rooms, books,

    in words and silence.

New Poems

Reflections at Forty-Nine

for Jean

Nothing is to be seen
in the pond water except alga
            and weed. The breeze is stiff,
    too stiff. The last leaves of summer
        float in ripple and eddy.

In the dusty window
of the summer place the sun of dusk
            glimmers. But behind it
    in the glass a shade passes, light
        trumps the eye. The sight winks out.

The bedroom is deckled with moon.
Shadow undresses in the mirror—
            the heft of a thick man
    in a thin frame. Night is sparing.
        The alarm keeps track of it.

But there is your dark eye.
The image there is clear. The leaves turn
            on the iris, the lash
    flickers. Yet no mistaking what
        we two see stealing away.

The Habitation

There is no way out.
Now the windows have begun
to cloud over: cobwebs, dust.
The stairs and floors are unstable—
the hours nibble the foundations.

In the bedrooms, sheets
have begun to yellow, spreads
to fray. Coverlets have worn
to the colors of late autumn,
thin as a draft sifting at the sill.

On the kitchen floor
crumbs and rinds lie recalling
the old feasts. In the larder
preserves rust among speckled jars;
the bins yawn; shadow sates the cupboards.

The fire has been damped
at the hearth: its bed of ash
sinks in pit-holes over brick.
The ceiling snows on the carpet—
Rejoice! Rejoice! The house is failing!

Vigilance

You stand waiting. You listen.
At your back the house is still,
between the tickings of clocks and timbers.
Beneath the rough soles of your feet
you can feel the cellar stretching to its foundations—
silence in the stone, the furnace brooding.

Shades are partly drawn against
the night. The panes are harder
than ice and as cold. Were you to touch them
they would shatter or seal you in.
The scent of dust is scattered in the air. The breathing
of the stairwell is a deep cascade. Now.

It will happen now: The knob
will turn, the tooth of the lock
take a strain in the cheek of the door where
it is set. You do not ask, "Who
is it?" It makes no mind; it is the wind of autumn,
the winterchase, the sky of change. The hours

flatten on the walls where you
have pinned them; you sense their weight
dragging in their frames against the wire.
A flake of plaster sifts onto
the carpet stretching like a lane of leaves along the
hall. You listen to the respiring rooms

where youth is dreaming age, where
aging sleeps. And you patrol,
you walk the hours listening to nibs scraping,
paper rattling, clocks marking. You
watch the knobs revolve, the windows shake, and in the flue
you hear the cinders rustling to the grate.

The Girl You Thought You Loved

Open the trunk: She is there,
   breathing—the girl you thought you loved.
These are her eyes, a pair of opals
      in a twist of tissue.

This is her heart, this dogged
   valentine knocking at the chest.
Who is she—who have you been, and where,
      and when? The spider locks

its web across this clock, this
   pendulum moving in the lace
billowing like her hair. The ticking
      of her bones on a bed

is ragged in the skull. Here
   is her scent: Dust in an attic,
a wasp buzzing. A sack of marbles
      rolls out the times of love.

Attic Poem

This is already old. When you find these pages
they will be brown as autumn. The ink
will look like bottled shadow etched
on a leaf. The attic room in which I write

will stand in these words only, if it stands, if it
ever stood. I see myself as I am now
as through an hourglass telescope reversed,
the falling sand turning the sight grainy

as a curled photograph: *The man writes*
in his house by the lake, in rainy weather,
his family asleep below—the two crones
and the ancient boy, his trucks scaled to rust.

That love is dead; all the trees are leaving.
It is spring; it is the fifth spring
since I was that other
not dreaming of a son:

It was as though he were a hollow fang
filled with midwinter and night. The bed was sweaty.
The ache was solid, without a sharp center.
He marveled that so much pain could keep him alive.

Sand is filling the attic room.
Leaves are turning in the night.
That love is dead, twice dead.
Darken it now. Close the book.

A Daughter Moves Out

for Melora

She has left
her posters on the wall.
The phone lies overextended on
the floor, humming: its
black panel is gone;
it shows its coils.

There are dust
bunnies under the bed.
The books on the yellow shelves study
the color brown—an
uncertain shade tilts
against the sun

falling down
into the winter lake.
Who, though, is this in the closet, hung
from a rack, his slit
eyes lidded in the
gloaming? Is it

the specter
of the prom-watcher, ghost
of the dawn-waiter, the hanger-on?
Yes, it is he who
clutches at glass, sand
siling out from

beneath his
feet, between his dry toes
into the lower cone. Let him wear
shadow, let him hang
on for a while.

Cancer

for John, in memoriam

We did not know, then, what the wen
    was on his heel. The gulls wheeled
in the summer sun, the combers
        broke and broke; the sand siled.
    On the beach the grandchild ran
    and stopped, dug wells, ran again

while the old man slept in a round
    shadow cast against the light.
The old wife dreamed beside his dream,
        wound in a shawl, as shade
    fretted the edge of waking.
    But all the while, as the tide

pulsed, moving by moments toward
    the drying seaweed of high
water, through the web of his veins
        the crab sidled, stalking.
    The day was perfect, then. Now
    a sea-change has taken it;

rather, it has become two days,
    that fair one and another
in which sandworms rise from the child's wells,
        segmented, mandibled.
    The beach umbrella sends its shade
    casting over the rising surf

to meet the east wind. The seabed
    is calm and murderous with
life. The boats toss like dreams, their nets
        seining the undertow.
    Now the ocean is almost
    upon us—our eyes are stars

    with spines; our minds are eight-armed; they
grope and coil in the darkness of the sun.

The Recurring Dream

for Luigi, in memoriam

I seek my father—that minister
of the deep—among the furniture
        of my childhood. I step out of waking
    into this room and know
that time has passed. The windows are webbed
    and moonstreaked. A lamp with a glass shade,

        green and saffron, burns
on a brass stem. The bookcases hold sermons
        and silence. My aquaria
    stand among tumbled
tomes and testaments. The dust rises
    into the amber darkness.

    I disturb a desert of hours,
search for the fish that glide
        in musty waters—blue scales
    glint under my glance,
their eyes are corals budding
    among rusty blades of sea grass

        and swordplants. I remove the glass lids
and dip my hand into the water—
        it is what I have feared:
    shadow of a shadow, dim air
flowing from corner to corner.
    The fish rise along the curtains

178

to swim about me in the air,
their black fins wavering.
    I dig in the gravel stranded
  among the shelving,
the decaying books. I dig,
    and here, in the root

  of the largest plant, blooming
from a socket of bone, I find my father
    where he has scuttled,
at last to be brought back, smiling.

Corral

for Christopher

When he was small I lay awake at night
    and dreamt of how I loved him
sleeping beyond the wall of lath and plaster,
    flesh and bone and blood that lay between us.

Now he's grown. Now, in half a year, he's gone
    from spore to weed taller than
the man who fathered him, the sire who lies
    dreaming his waking fictions of the dark—

that hobbyhorse of old, the rearing roan,
    the sorrel nag of nightmare
held at bay by words, and words alone like love
    that leap the wall to find the yearling flown.

Conceit

If I were you, I wouldn't listen
to me. If I stood there in your shoes,
staring at this graying man writing
in an attic late at night, a motor snoring
and music trickling from speakers
to seep through a sleeping house,

I would turn away, thinking of dreams
I have had, wondering if I'd have more
someday, some night, some winter morning,
the blue of the lake dripping out of its ice, wind
sniffing at the window. But spring
will have come by then. If you

were I you would be grateful. You'd say,
"Listen to that nib scratching, the grass
struggling up through drifts of sleep, these words
forming themselves as though they meant something to me."
You would say, "Over the chimney
of this house night is lifting

beneath the wings of geese returning
to their old haunts." And I would reply,
"They have never been away. All is
as it was, as it will always be." Then, shaking
your head, you would turn your back, you
would leave me here just as I

would leave you, if I were you walking
down the stairs, yellow light cascading
out of the ceiling, along the eaves,
into the rooms full of sleeping people whose love
will wash through our dreams of waking
when we shall lie down at last.

Poem

It is time to write a poem.
You have spun out the string of hours—
      it winds down the road, across
      people's lawns; it tangles itself
in the bushes of the park, catches
      in the lower limbs of a horse

      chestnut, and there, now, it lifts to
a kite, a blue kite against the gray
        sky. You must shinny after
      it. When you've caught it, hauled it down
by its rag tail, you see your poem
      scrawled on the tissue wrinkling in

      your hand. You feel the balsa rib
bow. Windcaught, the kite whispers free, sweeps
        across the street, blowing like
      the spiders that ride the air as
voyagers: you have read that somewhere;
      the kite spins out its line. You can

      not now follow. Your hands stop. No
longer do they climb and circle. You
        have seen the poem. The day
      freezes in its frame. The words squirm
out from beneath your hand. The wind is
      solid air, the clouds the color

of waiting. Only the kite moves
above the still neighbors in their rooms,
        on their lawns, amid their sounds
    turned to rosedust hovering in
a blank white square of world: When that is
    done, things will move again. The kite

    will be somewhere in the center
of the shifting web it is weaving.
        You will follow it, follow
    the filament from pause to pause,
poem to poem. It is almost
    done. You can feel the wind stirring.

A NOTE ABOUT THE AUTHOR

Lewis Turco teaches English and is the Director of the Writing Program at SUNY College in Oswego, New York. He is the author of *The Book of Forms: A Handbook of Poetics* (1968) and *Visions and Revisions of American Poetry* (1986), which received the Melville Cane Award from the Poetry Society of America for 1986, as well as eleven collections of poetry and five other books of criticism, bibliography, or instruction.